THIS BOOK BELONGS TO

_____

_____

_____

THE JOY OF
GARDENS

Roses
PIERRE-AUGUSTE RENOIR

*O*ne may live without bread but
not without roses.
Jean Richepin

*O*ne should learn also to enjoy the neighbour's garden,
however small; the roses straggling over the fence,
the scent of lilacs drifting across the road.
Henry Van Dyke

*F*lowers are the sweetest things God ever made…
Henry Ward Beecher

*I*n Eastern lands they talk in flowers,
And they tell in a garland their loves and cares;
Each blossom that blooms in their garden and bowers,
On its leaves a mystic language bears.
J.G. Percival

God Almighty first planted a garden;
and, indeed, it is the purest of human pleasures.
Francis Bacon

Yes, in the poor man's garden grow
Far more than herbs and flowers –
Kind thoughts, contentment, peace of mind,
and joy for weary hours.
Mary Howitt

It is so wrong to think of the beauty of flowers
only when they are at their height of blooming;
bud and half-developed flower,
fading blossom and seed pod are as lovely,
and often more interesting.
Clare Leighton

If I had but two loaves of bread,
I would sell one and buy hyacinths,
for they would feed my soul.
The Koran

Orchard: Woman and Barrow
CAMILLE PISSARRO

*I*t is good to be alone in a garden
at dawn of dark so that all its shy presences
may haunt you and possess you in a reverie
of suspended thought.
James Douglas

Camille and Jean Monet in the Garden at Argenteuil
CLAUDE MONET

The love of flowers is really the best teacher
of how to grow and understand them.
Max Schling

Gardening has compensations
out of all proportion to its goals.
It is creation in the pure sense.
Phyllis McGinley

Flowers often grow more beautifully on dung-hills
than in gardens that look beautifully kept.
Saint Francis de Sales

A modest garden contains,
for those who know how to look and wait,
more instruction than a library.
Henri Frederic Amiel

Yellow Fleur-de-lis
J.L. BRECK

*T*he soft south wind, the flowers amid the grass,
The fragrant earth, the sweet sounds everywhere,
Seemed gifts too great almost for man to bear.
William Morris

*T*ry to keep a garden beautiful to yourself alone
and see what happens – the neighbour,
hurrying by to catch his train of mornings,
will stop to snatch a glint of joy from the iris
purpling by your doorstep. The motorist will throw
on brakes and back downhill just to see those
Oriental poppies massed against the wall.
Nature is always on the side of the public.
Richardson Wright

*W*eather means more when you have a garden.
There's nothing like listening to a shower
and thinking how it is soaking in around
your lettuce and green beans.
Marcelene Cox

*W*e ought to be custodians, not owners;
it should be our privilege to help
the living things in our garden.
A really good man should want to tend
a garden, even if it is not his own;
this is the decisive test.
Clare Leighton

*W*hatever hour the sun may say,
It's always time for weeding;
The dandelion which blooms today
Tomorrow will be seeding.
A.A. Milne

*W*hen you have a garden you have a future
and when you have a future, you are alive.
Frances Hodgson Burnett

A garden is an awful responsibility.
You never know what you may be aiding to grow in it.
Charles Dudley Warner

The Little Gardener
FREDERIC BAZILLE

*T*he man who has planted a garden
feels that he has done something
for the good of the whole world.
Charles Dudley Warner

Woman Sewing
LUDOVIC VALLEE

I meant to do my work today
But a brown bird sang in an apple tree,
And a butterfly flitted across the field
And all the leaves were calling me.
Richard LeGallienne

*A*ll gardeners know better than other gardeners.
Chinese Proverb

*W*hat makes a garden
And why do gardens grow?
Love lives in gardens –
God and lovers know!
Carolyn Giltinan

*T*o create a little flower is the labour of ages.
William Blake

Lilacs
ALFRED JUERGENS

*B*ut each spring a gardening instinct,
sure as the sap rising in the trees, stirs within us.
We look about and decide to tame
another little bit of ground.
Lewis Gannet

*G*ardening is one of the rewards of middle age,
when one is ready for an impersonal passion,
a passion that demands patience, acute awareness
of a world outside oneself, and the power to keep
on growing through all the times of drought,
through the cold snows, towards those moments
of pure joy when all failures are forgotten
and the plum tree flowers.
May Sarton

*T*o a gardener there is nothing more exasperating
than a hose that just isn't long enough.
Cecil Roberts

*T*o sit in the shade on a fine day and look upon
verdure is the most perfect refreshment.
Jane Austen

*T*he best way to get real enjoyment
out of the garden is to put on a wide straw hat,
dress in thin loose-fitting clothes,
hold a trowel in one hand
and a cool drink in the other,
and tell the man where to dig.
Charles Barr

I think that if ever a mortal heard the voice of God
it would be in a garden in the cool of the day.
F. Frankfurt Moore

I have loved the feel of the green grass under my feet,
and the sound of the running stream by my side,
and the face of the fields has often comforted
me more than the faces of men.
John Burroughs

In the garden, Maurecourt
BERTHE MORISOT

O the green things growing, the green things growing,
The faint sweet smell of the green things growing!
I should like to live, whether I smile or grieve,
Just to watch the happy life of my green things growing.
Dinah M.M. Craik

Gladioli
CLAUDE MONET

M y jewels are in my garden,
And who can gauge their worth?
I look at them and feel myself
The richest man on Earth,

They're gems of priceless beauty,
Investments very rare,
With such jewels in my garden,
Am I not a millionaire?
J.M. Robertson

T he kiss of the sun for pardon,
The song of the birds for mirth,
One is nearer God's Heart in a garden
Than anywhere else on earth.
Dorothy Frances Gurney

A garden without its statue is like
a sentence without its verb.
Joseph W. Beach

Lady in a Garden
F.C. FRIESEKE

Gardening is creative work,
just as much as painting or writing a poem.
Hanna Rion

I know not which I love the most,
Nor which the comeliest shows,
The timid, bashful violet
Or the royal-hearted rose;
The pansy in her purple dress,
The pink with cheek of red,
Or the faint, fair heliotrope who hangs,
Like a bashful maid, her head.
Phoebe Cary

Flowers have a mysterious and subtle influence
upon the feelings, not unlike some strains of music.
They relax the tenseness of the mind.
They dissolve its rigor.
Henry Ward Beecher

Woman Digging in an Orchard
CAMILLE PISSARRO

The trouble with gardening is that it does not remain an avocation. It becomes an obsession.
Phyllis McGinley

The more one gardens, the more one learns; and the more one learns, the more one realizes how little one knows. I suppose the whole of life is like that: the endless complications, the endless difficulties, the endless fight against one thing or another, whether it be green-fly on the roses or the complexity of personal relationships.
Vita Sackville-West

Gardening should really be done in blinkers. Its distractions are tempting and persistent, and only by stern exercise of will do I ever finish one job without being lured off to another.
Richardson Wright

Chrysanthemums
CLAUDE MONET

I have noticed the almost selfish passion
for their flowers which old gardeners have,
and their reluctance to part with a leaf
or a blossom from their family.
They love the flowers for themselves.
Charles Dudley Warner

*O*ne of the most delightful things about a garden
is the anticipation it provides.
W.E. Jones

*M*ad fools of gardeners go out in the pouring rain
To prove they're Anglo-Saxon
They rarely put their macks on;
Each puts on rubber boots and squelches
through moist terrain,
Then leaves the mud and silt on
the Wilton.
Alan Melville

ALSO IN THIS SERIES

The Joy of Food and Drink
The Joy of Home
The Joy of Music

First published in Great Britain in 1998 by
JARROLD PUBLISHING LTD
Whitefriars, Norwich NR3 1TR

Developed and produced by
FOUR SEASONS PUBLISHING LTD
London, England

Text research by *Pauline Barrett*
Designed and typeset by *Judith Pedersen*

Printed in Dubai

Copyright © 1998 Four Seasons Publishing Ltd

All rights reserved.

ISBN 0 7117 1034 1

ACKNOWLEDGEMENTS

Four Seasons Publishing Ltd would like to thank all those
who kindly gave permission to reproduce the words and visual
material in this book. We would particularly like to thank Bridgeman Art
Library and Visual Arts Library for the use of pictures in their collections.

Front Cover: *Lady in a Garden* F.C. FRIESEKE
Visual Arts Library Library
Back Cover: *Monet's Garden at Giverny* JOHN BRECK
Visual Arts Library
Title Page: *Lady in a Garden* CLAUDE MONET
Visual Arts Library